The Essence of A Pearl

Written By:

Linda Diane Lay, Angelia Richhart, Amber Richhart,
Lay Family &
The Royal House of Normandy Royal Lay Family
Illustrator: Angelia Richhart

Books
By:

Lay Family Publishing

Poetic Colors

The Sugar Orchard

Divinely Guided:
Faith, Love, Hope, Peace & Joy

The Essence of A *Pearl*

Written By:

Linda Diane Lay, Angelia Richhart, Amber Richhart.
Lay Family &
The Royal House of Normandy Royal Lay Family
Illustrator: Angelia Richhart

Lay Family Publishing

The Essence of a Pearl
Copyright © 2016 Lay Family Publishing
Authors: Linda Diane Lay, Angelia Richhart, Amber Richhart, Lay Family, &
The Royal House of Normandy Royal Lay Family

Authors: Linda Diane Lay, Amber Richhart, Angelia Richhart, Lay Family &
The Royal House of Normandy Royal Lay Family
Illustrator: Angelia Richhart
Title: The Essence of a Pearl
Description: Volume of free verse poetry
Identifiers:
(Hardcover ISBN 978-1-300-43152-7) (Paperback ISBN: 978-1-300-16136-3)
(Paperback ISBN: 9798224146826) (E-book ISBN: 9798201589295)

Subjects: Classification BISAC (North America)
POE024000 POETRY / Women Authors
POE001000 POETRY / Anthologies (multiple authors)
POE005010 POETRY / American / General
POE023030 POETRY / Subjects & Themes / Animals & Nature

Lay Family Publishing
Published & Printed in the United States of America
10   9   8   7   6   5   4   3   2   1

Lay Family Publishing

Table of Contents

The Essence of
A
Pearl

Introduction

A single pearl to a string of pearls always encompasses so much beauty, rarity, and worth to me. Yet they require no cutting and no polishing by man. They are the only gems found and formed In a living creature. They can take up to four years to form. Many people tend to overlook the deeper meaning of a single pearl and its true essence and beauty. While a pearl represents integrity, serenity, and loyalty to some. A pearl represents God's wisdom gained through experience and understanding to me. Just like a pearl is formed around a piece of sand over time, we are molded and formed by how we perceive our life experiences. If we can learn to grow from our everyday experiences, whether good or bad. We could use the opportunities we have to reflect. We would learn powerful lessons that we could use to change our lives and those around us for the better. We always tend to grow the most when there is pressure on us, and we always tend to need Christ the most when everything is going wrong. Perhaps God is using the circumstances in your life to form a beautiful pearl.

Mathew 13:45-46

"Again, the kingdom of heaven is like a merchant
looking for fine pearls."
"When he finds one of great value, he went away and
sold everything he had and bought it."

Jesus Christ gave his life up for you because you are of
great worth to him.
He bought and paid for all your sins.
He loves you more than you will ever know.

Love Letters

Eternal Flame

The sweet tender kiss of a love so dearly missed,
to the poetic passions of a love not fully expressed.

From the heartfelt warmth of a handheld kiss,

to the unshaken foundation of love's sheer bliss.

From a lover's eternal flame to the heartache of a

love that was lost,

all-consuming dull pain.

From being so blissfully young and naïve.

To never fully understanding why love makes us

grieve.

From being in an all-consuming love worthwhile,

and engaging in love's sweet, sympathetic smiles.

A Woman's Heart

Golden nova's can light up a darkened night sky,

just the same as love can lighten up a lonely soul's

cry.

A golden heart is not meant to rip and tear,

just as a woman's heart should be gently handled

with care.

A Love Song

I hear the sparrows chirping their sweet spring chimes,

as I walk through the rose garden that is covered in

vines.

The sparrows and doves have found their mate,

and are nesting nearby the garden's gates.

I see the sun rising as I look toward the east,

as I felt the warmth of the sun upon my unsandaled

feet.

I followed a dirt path that led to the fountains.

As I could see in the distance.

The earth's beautiful array of mountains.

Passion

True love is like a flame that burns so bright.

It ignites the heart's passion,

throughout the night.

Loving Embrace

The moon is at its highest peak tonight.

With a shadowy light gleaming down,

piercing through my window and my silk-laced

gown.

I was in hopes to find my lover,

but he could not be found.

But the hint of honey suckles still lingered all around.

As I slowly walked across the floor to latch thy

swaying door,

I could feel a cool breeze rushing in from the night's

ocean-roaring winds.

I felt your gentle touch, which made me turn around.

As you grasped me with your loving arms,

I knew I had been found.

Loving Kiss

A simple hug and a loving kiss are life's true

pleasures and simply bliss.

Ever After Bliss

From the oceans loud, watery roars,
to the heartache of a lover who was so bitterly

scorned.

From the sweet and tender kiss upon a rosy cheek,

to the heartfelt secrets so many of us keep.

From the bittersweet locket around one's neck,

to the unforgettable memories they will never

forget.

From a secret diary with a lock and key,

to the memorable moments of love being so free.

From your first kiss when you were so young and

considerably naive,

to your ever-after bliss and your lives being

interweaved.

Timing of Love

So many hearts are lonely,

lost in this life's time.

Simply living day by day,

and always rushing loves time.

A Big Heart

Having a big heart is good for the soul,

because it brings a wealth of understanding to the

once unknown.

Destined Love

An all-consuming love that is intertwined with fate,

is always on time and it is never late.

Our path is prewritten,

or so it seems.

The only thing we need is love,

because it will set us free.

One True Love

I stare at the glistening stars and moon at night,

under the moonlight's soft forbidden light.

Standing on the balcony,

hidden by night.

Hoping you could hold me so very tight.

I searched for you, my desire, my dove.

You are my one desire,

my one true love.

I have grown so lonely since you been gone,

my heart wishes it were not so terribly long.

You ignited a flame that melted my heart,

that watered my existence from the start.

Like the cool drizzling rains of spring,

that seeps into the earth and always sings.

My heart burns brighter than the light of day,

with the simple yet romantic words that you say.

Lock and Key

Life is so short and yet so sweet,

why do we keep our hearts desires under lock and

key?

Life is a true mystery,

I think we all can agree.

A Beautiful World

You never knew I existed until the day I met you,

but you changed my life in so many beautiful ways.

I wish I could thank you!

You gave me hope in the future,

you gave me hope in myself.

You made me see all the beauty in the world,

that I could not see myself.

The End of Time

I love the sugar upon your lips,

the sweet-smelling taste that I can no longer resist.

You placed your lips gently upon mine,

as my heart grew weak with love.

I will love you,

until the end of time.

Remembering When

Your lips are like cream,

so tender and sweet.

Like the beauty of a luscious, ripened peach.

Your heart brings warmth to my very soul,

although this life has taken so many tolls.

Your love is what I thirst for,

through these darkened days.

As I can remember your touch in so many beautiful

ways.

As I daydream with my loving thoughts,

I remember the days when we would just sit and

talk.

These things I remember are so refined,

remind me of when our lives had better times.

The Beholder

Love is so hard to find,

when you're looking for a beautiful mind.

Unfailing Love

Over the mountains in a summery bliss,

I see my true love!

whom I have so dearly missed.

Over the years that has slowly gone by,

I'm so glad that I had you by my side.

Distant Memories

When I walk the trail that passes the railroad ties

and travel the path under the bridge.

I still remember my first love,

when we were just mere kids.

Always laughing and playing tag.

If we had only stayed together,

Imagine the life we would have had.

First Kiss

Being young and naive is truly bliss,

especially when you receive your first love's kiss.

A True Love

The loving rays of dawn's first light,

to the cool darkened breeze of a starry night.

With the warm embraces of a lover's tale,

to the first written love letters read upon a secret

trail.

Love being so beautiful, yet so frail.

Makes love worthwhile like the holy grail.

Many will search for it,

yet so few will find.

A true love that can withstand the test of time.

From a lover's embrace to a sensual kiss,

true love is worthwhile and is life's true bliss.

Essence of Love

The sweet aroma of your lingering presence,

makes my heart weak with your sensual essence.

I was wanting more,

my heartfelt confession.

I adorned your love,

my secret obsession.

Timeless Love

True love nourishes the soul and makes love

worthwhile.

Like couples taking a stroll through life's many miles.

For better or worse,

they'll always be there.

Because in your heart,

you know they truly care.

Warmth of Love

Love can warm the heart, the soul, and the mind.

It can even warm a home,

if it's given enough time.

Endless Love

For my heart longs to have you,

forever in my arms.

To not ever knowing how you seduced me with your

empathetic charm.

From loving your lips to your gradual touch,

I will always love you...

No matter the distance, no matter the time.

No matter how much I miss you,

it'll be until the end of time.

Soulmate

Love is everlasting,

like the stars above.

I wish I could find my one true love.

Loves Passion

You're like a sweet aroma of perfume that indulges

my senses.

With the romantic gestures and words that you say,

my beating heart could never stray.

I can only hope in this newfound love,

I am blessed with such treasure

of

an undying love.

Consoling Moments

Love is always feeling within your

heart, mind, and soul.

Love is also always knowing in my heart,

that you will be there to console.

The Moonlight

Fishing in the moonlight for life and for love.

Fishing in the moonlight with my prayers above.

Fishing in the moonlight,

my heart can feel your tug.

Fishing in the moonlight,

I will never underestimate this love.

Love Lessons

People tend to view love as if it always ends in pain.

Only if you could open your eyes,

would you truly see love.

For there is so much to be gained.

Embracing Love

The lonely, saddened tears rolling down one's face,

to the uplifting joy of a loved one's embrace.

Days pass by as the seasons forever change.

Just as the ocean tides have always been sustained.

To the beloved echoes of a loved one's laugh,

always reminds us to never forget our past.

To love is to learn, just as to live is to love.

But we shall never forget our blessings from above.

Memories

Down by the seashore on the silvery sand,

I walk with my lover,

hand in hand.

As the crisp ocean tides roll upon this ancient land,

I can feel the water immerse itself into the silvery

sand.

Leaving our footprints in the midst of our past.

But, always remembering what we have always had.

A Lover's Embrace

A lover's embrace with bodies intertwined,

a veil made of lace with a meeting of minds.

A sweet-smelling taste of a lover of mine.

Love is never too late,

it's a pleasurable find.

Missed Love

Somehow,

in the wintery midst.

I see my true love,

that I have so dearly missed.

As the snowflakes fall from the darkened night sky,

I never want to say goodbye.

Life's Essence

Rose Petals

Rose petal blossoms in the garden of Eve,

that blankets the floor with their quilt pattern

weave.

With the sweet and alluring fragrance of the day lily

blossoms,

to the tall-enchanted pillars that surround the

garden columns.

To the cascading white petals of the beautiful

Magnolia,

who is secretly as beautiful and as sweet as our skies

golden nova's.

To the sacred sentimental petals of the Dalila,

that constantly flow like the rivers of Italia.

Golden Fields

As I walk through golden fields of wheat and grain,

I can hear the birds sing their melodies before the

rains.

Truly Beautiful

This life is truly beautiful,

yet so many choose not to see.

Just like this world's beautiful, majestic roaring seas.

The whispers of the wind's divinity,

that turns into a breeze.

That sweeps across my neckla'ce that no one else

can see.

Or the beautiful warmth of the sun's glistening rays

that bring forth life,

in the midst of a darkened day.

This life is truly beautiful,

I hope you don't wait to see.

All of this world's beautiful miracles,

and to truly be free

The Meaning of Life

When you grow old and acquire much age,

you no longer keep your heart trapped in a cage.

You free yourself from all the burdens of this life,

because you finally realize the meaning of life.

Gods Hand

The stars in the galaxies were placed in the universe

by God's hands,

always tend to fail the understanding of man.

We search for all the answers,

but will never fully understand.

All the things that were never created by man.

We claim we created life in its majestic form.

Yet,

we cannot reverse death and all its thorns.

Truly Free

If you know who you are,

you are truly free.

Just like the flowering blossoms of the sugar

orchards humming bees.

Thy blossoms never speak or have deliberate

thoughts.

Yet,

they know the time is coming for them to produce

thy crops.

Thy bees are always busy gathering thy nectar of life,

humming with innocence,

and becoming bearers of new life.

These things are truly simple,

yet so fascinating to see.

If you could only open your eyes, you could truly see.

A Secret Garden

A secret garden with a fruitful essence,

brings forth beauty and an alluring presence.

Where time seems to stop and is an eternity long.

The sweet aroma of the blossoms,

sings their gentle song.

Blue Array

I walked along the seashore in the coolness of

dawn's first light,

I could see the waves crashing with their grip held so

tight.

Within the waters of the oceans,

there is a blue array.

I could feel the emotions of the ocean,

as it began a new day.

Always knowing and always turning tides.

It seemed to hold so many secrets,

you only got to wish you knew in time.

Star Gazing

The galaxies are so brisk,

hidden beyond the night's skies.

Even though we night gaze,

hoping to understand life.

We are truly so very simple and yet so very small.

Entangled in this life's mysteries,

and stargazing at the night's skies in awe.

Night of July

Cardinals that fly so effortlessly in the sunlit sky,

to the bluebirds that are nesting their eggs in the

night of July.

From the night owls hooting their sovereign cries,

to the brindled feathered hawks that encompass the

darkened night skies.

From dark till dawn, we hear the chirping songs of a

world not yet known.

That holds its mysteries like a fortune untold.

The Gift of Life

We are interwoven so uniquely and yet so defined,

in the woman's womb who bore us into this mystical

life.

Never fully understanding the complexities of this

life,

and always raising the question of why we were

given life.

Season's Secrets

The crumbling leaves upon the forest floor,

to the sun's glistening waves upon the ocean shore.

From the snow-glistening flakes falling from the sky,

to the warmth of a spring day bearing new life.

From the warm and embracing breeze of a summer's

eve,

to the colored-filled foliage falling from the trees.

From the glistening dew, resting upon a blade of

grass.

To the sound of the oceans roar,

always remembering its' past.

From the peaks of the highest mountains simmering

secrets,

to the sandy floors,

unkept secrets

Spring

When the first green tender shoots appear,

you always know that spring is surely near.

For the earth is thirsty to come back to life,

always in the perfect precision of time.

From the spring's evening days to the misting rains,

that will yield new life in the desert plains.

Gods Heart

When you are down on your luck,

and you don't think you can make it through.

Don't forget to look up,

because I have never forgotten you!

You mean more to me than the stars, the moon, and

the trees!

So why is it that you have so easily forgotten me?

Heartbreaking Moments

Thorns and Thistles

Thorns and thistles surround my very heart,

I grow them there on purpose to protect my

beating heart.

My heart was shattered into pieces and scattered

into the wind,

from all the times you left me and broke me,

over and over again.

You pierced my heart with grief,

as I always wanted more.

But you were never there for me,

even though you swore.

My heart was broken into pieces,

but never again, no more.

For you were never there for me,

and my heart can take no more.

The False Mask

When a man breaks your heart,

yet rips it in half.

Is there anything left other than his false mask?

Meant For Love

Her heart was meant for love,

she had always intended it that way.

She gave it to a man who blindfolded her and pretended he would

stay.

She never questioned his actions or why he chose to leave.

She just accepted the fact that it was not meant to be.

He brought her to her knees,

where he thought she could not rise.

He ripped out her beating heart with all his ruthless lies.

Then he left her in the dark,

where she would eventually start to cry.

For what she did not know was,

he would soon be back again.

But this time when he came, she was already gone.

He couldn't even find the blindfold he had put on.

He couldn't understand how she could have possibly left,

until he looked in the mirror and met the man she had met.

Reflection

As I stare at my reflection,

in the glass-fogged-covered mirror.

I remember how my heart is drowning,

in sad and lonely tears.

Mere Task

I understand completely why you wore a false mask,

it was because you were incomplete and looked at

me as no more than a mere task.

Loving Truth

All the tears you cried gradually flowed down your

cheeks,

for just one second you felt overwhelmingly weak.

You broke down in tears, never letting anyone know.

The heartache that you felt,

came from your very own soul.

Perhaps it was from the man you thought you had

known?

He never said goodbye; he just walked out and left.

Leaving you in shackles, as you continuously wept.

You slowly grew stronger as the days seemed to

pass.

Learning who you were and then regretting your

past.

You finally grew up and found the key.

Knowing that it was the truth that would set you

free.

Unrequited Love

As I stare at a ring and all my dreams that you broke.

I realized you were my unrequited love,

and a very sad joke.

A Woman's Tears

Fairytales and bliss upon your sweet-tender lips.

To the sugar-coated lies,

that led to my heart's demise.

These things you remember,

yet never truly forget.

Is one reason why so many women have wept.

Mirror Image

You mirrored me to make me believe you were the

one.

Then the mirror broke,

and your reflection was gone.

Illusions

You left my mind in a mystic haze,

after you seduced me with your delusional games.

Unpleasant Fruit

The fruit that you bear is unpleasant and unripe.

Even though when I first met you,

I thought you were my type.

When I took the first bite,

I instantly knew.

The bitter and sour taste you left in my soul,

would be hard to remove.

Tears

You fed on her tears and broken heart,

as if this pleased you.

You lapped up her salty tears as if a dog laps up

water.

Even still,

you could not quench your thirst.

Words Spoken

A broken heart seems as if it cannot be mended,

just as a sharp tongue can seem so wicked.

It is a double-edged sword with the words that we

speak,

because some bring life,

yet others bring grief.

Love vs. Hate

Love is never hate,

why is it that you cannot relate?

True Love's Worth

Hopeless romantic is what they tend to say.

But is it really hopeless,

when all they wanted was for a love to stay?

Through thick and thin,

or for better or worse.

Sadly,

this world will never cherish

true love's worth.

Tearful Eyes

To find someone true and faithful is truly a hard find.

Especially when we live in a day of ages,

where life brings so many tears to so many eyes.

The Remnant Sky

I stare at the silky gray clouds,

whose remnants are still attached to the sky.

Wondering if I'll catch a glimpse of a star shining

through the night sky.

Never understanding and never knowing why,

I let my heart seep into the emotions of the

darkened night sky.

As I grasp the chain necklace that hung around my

neck.

I try to wipe away the tears,

that I have sadly wept.

Cold Hearted

When you feel the pain that gnaws at your soul,

from a past lover who was always so bitterly cold.

Covered in ice and unbearably cold,

you finally realized you were with a man who lacked

a soul.

Hate & Pain

Instead of loving her,

you gave her hate and pain.

Instead of kissing her,

you pushed her away.

She cried a tear,

as it ran down her face.

You should have been there,

to wipe it from her face.

Remorse & Sorrow

You hovered over her remorse and sorrow,

as if it were a delightful delicacy.

Just waiting to be devoured.

The Past

To live is to love,

yet love feels like death.

Why is it when we are old,

we always regret our past?

Stained Glass

The stained-colored glass,

reminds me of all the emotions I once had felt for

you.

From the haunting memories to the daunting reality,

that I no longer feel these things for you.

They are just sheets of glass,

stained with the emotions I once wore.

Reminding me of all the tears

that washed away all these things,

that ate at my soul's core.

Blindfolded Love

Your lips spoke so many lies,

while your heart still had its previous ties.

Even though your lips kissed mine,

I could feel that your heartbeat for your past only.

I just chose not to see,

I was hoping that I could somehow make you

relinquish your past.

Heartbroken

Brittle and shattered into pieces is how he left you.

With no reconsideration,

this was not how he found you.

Nothing New

You always had a circle of hosts that were waiting

for you.

In the beginning,

I never understood why this was so important to

you.

Until my heart was broken then tore into threads,

you tried to tie me with.

This is when I realized,

you were not a one-woman man.

But this was nothing new to you.

Shadow

Light casts no shadow,

there is no darkness within.

The only things that cast a shadow,

are those things with sin.

Secret Tears

When you come to a home

and find it unraveled and unkept.

You come to the conclusion,

that there have been secrets and tears that have

been wept.

Broken

When your heart is weak, but your soul is strong,

you always wonder how love can go so terribly

wrong.

When you try your best,

but it wasn't enough.

Instead of loving you,

he craved another woman's love.

Full of Hate

If a man hates himself, he will hate his life.

In the coming days,

he will hate his wife.

He will become hollow, lacking a heart.

Full of envy and grief,

it will tear them apart.

Lost Love

My heart feels so lonely because you are no longer

here.

I do not understand why you were taken,

it was my biggest fear.

I feel so empty and lonely inside,

because you are no longer here to hold my hand at

times.

Or even wipe the tears from my saddened eyes.

I must travel this path without you,

which is my biggest fear.

You will always be in my memories,

and you will always be in my heart.

Even though I feel,

that we are an eternity apart.

The Railroads Path

I always seem to take the same old path,

past the railroad tracks.

Always wondering what could have been,

if only I had chosen to stay with him.

Memories

As I walk through my memories and realize my past.

Some things I will never understand,

why they didn't last.

Pearlie

I had a baby girl,

whose name was Pearlie.

She was not a human child,

she was a little Yorkie.

She was so dear and sweet,

just like a little child.

I loved her unconditionally,

as she always made me smile.

The day I lost her,

my heart was ripped in two.

For she was my baby girl,

and I shall always miss you.

Untold Truths

Yearning Heart

Some hearts yearn for more than this life can truly

give.

Not the materialistic things,

but to truly live.

We bridge the gap between our minds and our

hearts.

Never knowing the full distance,

this is what sets us apart.

There are three things that are true about love,

It takes all your body, soul, and mind to fully love.

Without these three things,

there is nothing to be gained.

For why do you think falling in love always ends in so

much pain?

Choose Love

Love is so simple,

yet always free to give.

Why do so many people hate each other,

and refuse too truly live?

Lust vs. Love

His lust is never love,

just a physical expression of his body.

If he is in love with your mind,

he will fall in love with your body.

If words fall from his lips that are empty and not

whole,

don't let him drink or sip from the cup of love that

you so dearly hold.

For if you do and give in too soon,

he will become drunk on desire only until the break

of dawn.

You will go out in search of him,

but he will be gone.

A Shallow Mind

A broken heart cannot be mended.

Like that of a shallow conscience,

is truly unforgiving.

Mystery

Never understanding the density of our galaxies

time,

just like never understanding the thoughts of a

materialistic mind.

You could have everything you ever wanted and

never be fulfilled,

but no one tends to believe this and thinks it's

surreal.

True Treasures

Everything that glitters is not always gold.

Just like the true treasures of life,

are only found when we are old.

Grandfather Clock

What is time?

But a passing of our momentary moments.

We cannot help but count our time on the hands of

a clock.

Wishing it by, even though it never really stops.

We wish it by through the hardest of our times.

Always asking the question of

Why? Why? Why?

But when we are happy and our lives are going

great.

You never really ponder the question of your fate.

Only in those moments do you feel weak and alone,

is when you sit and you ponder.

Are you really alone?

Gift of Life

As you grow older,

your heart begins to learn.

Each day is a gift,

and to not so endlessly yearn.

From The Heart

Why are there so many regrets that live in our

hearts?

When couples first meet,

nothing can tear them apart.

As time goes by,

they slowly drift apart.

Perhaps it is from the wedges they created,

with the hateful words that they say.

As time goes by,

everything seems to fall away.

Maybe it could have been different,

if only they chose loving words to say.

Always speak from the heart, and not from hate.

Life's too short to regret what we say.

Cutting Words

Never say words that you will later regret,

words that you wish never left your lips.

For our time here is short and our words can cut,

never drink from this poisonous cup.

Gardener

A farmer sows so many seeds and if it falls on fertile

soil,

it will grow indeed.

Whether it is a beautiful rose or thistles and thorns,

what you water with your mind is what your heart

adorns.

Your Perspective

Life is so short,

yet can be so full of life.

But many people retort this,

and choose to believe lies.

Human Life

People tend to believe that humans are the superior

beings.

Why is it yet,

we are so naive?

People choose hate rather than love,

yet hate leads to nothing more than a grudge.

There are three things that can diminish a life,

greed, envy, and hate, they all create strife.

For love is so simple and easy to give,

it can even replenish a soul's will to live.

Faith, Love & Hope

Faith is always knowing,

love is truly sacred and

hope is a loving promise.

The Hourglass

Always make time to enjoy your life.

For one day you'll blink,

and it'll have done passed you by.

Like sand in the hourglass, passing through.

Moments become distant memories,

yet this is true.

Gifts of Life

When you finally understand

all of life's most precious gifts.

You realize how short life

truly is.

What's Your Motive?

What is a motive but a simple thought of what one

plans to do?

For the goodwill of a man or the downfall of a man,

it is completely up to you.

For what one plans and conjures in his conspiring

thoughts,

soon becomes his reality and soon becomes his lot.

For what you do to others,

will always be repaid.

So, remember these words.

It all depends on you,

and how your actions will be swayed.

Wise Words

What are wise words

other than the mere thoughts of a man.

But when we speak from the heart,

it seems as though man can never understand.

A Giving Heart

People tend to take advantage of a person with a

truly giving heart.

Never expecting them to be all that truly smart.

But when you stand your ground,

is when they'll fall away.

But they'll always come back,

but for you there is not much to be gained.

So do a good deed,

for it is a just and upright thing to do.

But do not fall into the trap of continuously being

used.

Lessons

Life is a composition of lessons learned slowly over

time,

that always seems to raise our factual reasonings of

why.

Karma

To lie through your teeth,

is no more than empty words.

To cover the truth with filth and regret,

never underestimating yourself until you have no

one left.

But where lies are poured out,

It only brings forth illusions and deceit.

But the harbinger of the lies,

is the only one usually being deceived.

Because the truth will always prevail,

and I do believe this to be true.

For whatever you put forth,

usually always comes back to you.

Will Love Unfold?

Love is never meant for more than two souls.

For if a man is with more than one woman,

love can never unfold.

For if a man is with two women,

and claims he loves both.

This is no more than a lie,

and a false claim to boast.

Life Changes

People, places, and things will always seem to

change.

For life is always in a state of metamorphosis,

and so are you.

Love's Never Hate

Love is never hate,

this is a truly unfulfilling slate.

Compassion and love are always overflowing,

but so many people are always left unknowing.

Like a healing word,

it can heal so many broken hearts.

But hate breaks into resentment,

and tears us all apart.

A Simple Embrace

For a broken promise,

can lead to the shedding of many tears.

But a simple embrace can save you from loneliness

and despair.

Reflecting Thoughts

If you have a pure heart

yet,

someone always questions your motives or your

thoughts.

Do them a favor,

turn your back and walk.

Do not even chatter, let alone even talk.

For it is useless for you,

for their reflecting their own corrupt thoughts.

The Test of Time

Never be sad, depressed, or lonely,

for you are never truly alone.

This is just a physical test here,

until we all go back home.

Men and Women

Men seem to be born to fight and protect,

where women are born to nest and reflect.

Men tend to fight for their heart's desires,

whether it's money, a legacy, or an empire.

But when it comes to women, it is usually no more than a sexual desire

For their hearts are weak and their lust is strong.

But as for women, this scenario is usually wrong.

For a woman tend to love unconditionally so,

and she would never lust for another man unless her heart was broken

so.

If you win her heart, what a treasure it is to be found.

For she'll never leave your side,

and she'll be with you through life's ups and downs.

Blossom

A bud blossoms into a flower,

and friendship blossoms into love.

Passion & Obsession

Why do people get so obsessed?

To comfort themselves in worldly bliss,

or to try to find themselves all over again.

While their deepest passions lie within,

but passions are a humble and loving truth.

Where obsession will leave you utterly confused.

True Knowledge

For so many people thirst for worldly things.

Never understanding,

none of these things will ever remain.

Legacy

A man's life is his legacy and this is known,

the fruit of his endeavors will always be shown.

When he travelled the path of broken hearts and

tears,

he left all alone.

He will finally come to the realization,

his legacy was his home.

Blessed

Remember how truly blessed you are,

that you have life indeed.

For when we look back on our lives,

You'll realize it was a masterpiece.

Like an artist with a brush,

or a gardener with a seed.

You do not wish to rush these things,

for one day you will truly see.

A Seed of Change

As the petals fall from the flower's stem,

the seeds of change lie within.

To make a new start,

we must begin again.

Actions vs. Words

When you look at a man's or a woman's actions,

and not yet their words.

You tend to see the individual's true sense of worth.

For words can be hollow, always promising bliss.

Leading to sorrow and a love that was missed.

Worldly Thirst

The thirst for empowerment can never be quenched,

just like a burning fire that continues to be relit.

These things were mentioned years ago,

but no one understands the parables that were once

told.

For if you could control your hunger,

you would eventually see.

That there are many more things,

like life and love,

that are far more important to reach.

The Poor Man

A poor man is better than a rich man in so many

ways.

The poor man was poor,

because he gave all his riches away.

A Virtue

What is virtue?

A higher truth.

A simple understanding.

Lessons learned in our youth when we are young
and naïve.

Perhaps it is our destined path we choose,

no matter what we pretend not to see.

I do believe morals with the highest respect and
regard for life,

tend to be a virtue to me.

The Little Things

Some people look for answers to questions that

cannot be found,

instead of appreciating the little things that are so

beautifully renowned.

Life's Mysteries

A seed planted in an open heart,

produces a long-lasting love that you cannot tear apart.

From friendship to lovers to lovers and friends.

There are many things on this earth you'll never fully understand.

Whispers and chatter in a secret place,

only produces grudges and ends in hate.

From knowing the truth to understanding a lie,

there are many mysteries on this earth that you cannot deny.

From holding a hand to sharing a kiss,

tends to create a love that leads to bliss.

From being so young to slowly growing old,

many of life's mysteries are left untold.

From being full of folly to becoming very wise,

many of these life's mysteries are only understood in time.

The Truth Prevails

The truth is all love, and I tell you this.

Where hate is no more than deceitfulness.

So therefore,

love the truth and retort a lie.

For all these things seem to work themselves out in

time.

The truth will always prevail,

whereas I do believe a lie will always fail.

Trust

Never trust someone who cannot trust you,

there will always be their lust for others and

reoccurring disputes.

Helping Hand

Many people love to brag about life, their money,

homes, cars, and class,

but these people in my thoughts will always come

last.

For there are many people who cannot lift a hand to

help their mother, daughter, let alone a homeless

man.

This world is cold and hard to understand,

but this life is temporary try to understand.

A loving heart and a giving hand,

can save so many lives.

It is truly in your hands.

The Wind

Some people always expect you to be there for

them,

but when you need them the most they're gone with

the wind.

Men and Morals

A man with morals has an unfathomable will to

stand for the truth,

but morals to man with a boy's intellect is no more

than empty reasoning.

Flawed

If you did not see a person's physical beauty,

yet seen all their flaws.

Would you still be interested in them,

despite it all?

The Path

If you could see an individual's path and the life they

have lived until now,

would you still scoff and laugh with your

predisposed thoughts?

Or would you begin to question how?

Bleak World

People's hearts and eyes will always grow bleak,

especially in a world where there are so many that

are subconsciously weak.

Perspectives on Life

When you are so young and naive,

life seems like a beautiful mystery.

But...

When you grow old and grieve,

life seems like a tragic misery.

Forgotten Song

Living life in the moment with no regrets,

makes men and women in their old age reflect.

Did I live right?

or

Did I live wrong?

Tends to be their forgotten song.

One Thousand Miles

If you walked a thousand miles in someone else's

shoes,

maybe you could understand the will of their life and

the decisions that they choose.

Words

Blood is thicker than water,

is what they tend to say.

Although blood can cut deeper,

depending on what they say.

Assumptions

The ignorance of a man is always based on his

assumptions,

so never assume anything.

Otherwise,

your assumptions could consume you.

Lost In Time

Some hearts are lost in time,

this is true for so many.

Dwelling in the past,

but living in the present time.

This is so true for so many.

Family

Family is like a chain that can never be broken,

we are all interlocking in this life.

A Mother's Love

A mother's love is so pure and kind,

she will love you forever till the end of time.

Her heart is golden,

and she will hold you tight.

She will always teach her children

what is wrong and what is right.

Upright Father

A father stands so tall and strong,

always knowing right from wrong.

He teaches his children his morals and his truth,

the same golden rules he learned in his youth.

A Sister's Love

A sister's love is so unique,

and in so many ways she makes you feel complete.

With her silly jokes and her heartwarming stories,

a sister's love is like a beautiful journey.

She will even tell you a few heartfelt confessions,

but at the end of the day she's

your biggest blessing.

A Healing Heart

Photographs

A lot of people's stories are always left untold,

but maybe it is because this world has grown so very

cold.

To know these people's stories,

is to know their beating heart.

To know these people's stories,

is to know their very thoughts.

To know the stories behind a photo,

is sometimes left untold.

But there are so many stories that I wish I could

unfold.

Brother

A brother's shoulder is something to lean on,

through life's many trials.

They never show weakness,

throughout life's many miles.

They're always there to comfort your heart,

a sister and a brother can never be torn apart.

.

Life's Reflections

A bitter person reflects on the dark side of life,

with no one ever knowing their true reason why.

They tend to hoard grudges,

because they learned life's mysteries a little too late.

There is nothing here that lasts forever,

nor is it truly ever yours.

Your just borrowing time.

However,

a bitter heart endures.

If they could only open their eyes,

they could truly see.

All of life's miracles could set them free.

Life is So Delicate

Some people believe that love can set their lives

free,

where others tend to believe why are all these things

happening to me?

Our lives are confusing,

yet so beautiful to me.

When you think of the simplicity of our emotions,

and how deep they truly run.

You'll realize how delicate our lives and emotions

truly are.

Pages of Life

If your life were like the pages of an already written

book,

would you ever go back and rewrite some of your

pen ink strokes?

Trust in Him

People tend to lack emotions in this ever-growing,

cold world.

They become bitter with grief and dismay at their

sad and lonely broken hearts.

People in this world will always cause you pain.

So place your trust in the Lord,

for your life will be regained.

Love Life

So, I will remind you...

Do not forget to love your life,

because you are only blessed with one.

It is so much better to spend your days in

appreciation than dissatisfaction.

So, no matter how many trials and heartaches you

have had.

Just remember,

this life is too short to stay sad.

God's Hands

When you tend to look at the patterns and lines

embedded in your hands.

You seem to get a glimpse of this life,

and understand it is all in

God's hands.

Bend or Break

Hardships and trials will everyone meet,

the outcome always depends on whether you are

strong or weak.

For if you are strong,

you will overcome many things.

But for a weak individual,

they usually fail for the words that they say.

"I can't do it"

or

"I'm never enough."

When you decide to change your mind,

is when you'll overcome.

For strength,

it is a decision you subconsciously make.

Will you bend or will you break?

Love's Lessons

Love is never hate,

nor do these two things ever collide.

For if it were ever true love we speak of,

hate could never reside.

Hate is not even the opposite of love,

For this I do believe is a fact.

For in the absence of love grows grief,

but our hearts are still intact.

Starting Over

Some people try to know the future and only time

can tell,

they have so many wishes and hopes for their lives

to be swell.

But if you want to know the future,

look inside your heart.

For God is the one who will determine where you

should make a new start.

A Simple Message

As the leaves in the trees blow so effortlessly in the wind,

our lives will always unfold in a certain direction not known by man.

For our path in life is one step at a time,

slowly going through the motions, as it slowly passes us by.

For our dreams and our hopes are only truly known by God,

just as he is the only one who truly knows our hearts.

For us to find ourselves and the true meaning of life,

this can only be accomplished when we hold on to the divine.

For when our hearts decide to listen,

there is so much to be gained.

But sometimes this simple message is a lifetime away.

So, when you hear his voice and the softening of your heart,

never turn away because this is where your life will truly start.

He Saves The Lost

There was a man who was crucified on a cross,

his only reason for coming was to save the lost.

His hands and feet were pierced with sinful nails,

He went through this suffering to save you from hell.

He paid the price in full to free you from your bonds.

His heart is fully open,

if you receive him with open arms.

It is never too late to start over,

just give your life to him.

His love endures forever,

and he saved you from your sins.

A-Men

Dedication

This book is dedicated to all our family, friends, and

everyone we hold dear to our hearts.

But mostly, this book is dedicated to our

Lord and Savior,

Jesus Christ.

About The Authors

Linda Diane Lay, Angelia Richhart, and Amber Richhart are poets, writers, and authors of multiple great books. They reside in Indiana and have a love for poetry and the arts.

They have written an inspirational book named "Divinely Guided," which surrounds and entails the subjects of faith, love, hope, peace, and joy. While this book offers an inspirational message of love and acceptance through Jesus Christ, this book is based on Christianity and love. It is a good read for anyone wanting to learn more about Christianity, and to deepen their faith, and to strengthen their relationship with Christ.

They have also written three poetic books that are anthologies, which are collections of poems from each author compiled together in one beautiful work, such as "The Sugar Orchard," "Poetic Colors," and "The Essence of a Pearl." These books dive deep into the depths of femininity and the emotions that women feel throughout life, such as love, joy, and bliss, as well as exploring the sad poetic symphonies of pain, grief, and loss. These books have words that will touch your heart and soul, as well as offering beautifully hand-drawn images to separate each unique chapter.

The words in these books encompass wisdom, heartache, love, and grief that we have all felt throughout our lives. The words they use reflect such deep emotions that you will have cried the tears they have shed and shared the joy and feel as if you have encountered these life experiences yourself.

Linda Diane Lay, Angelia Richhart, and Amber Richhart use such passion and poetic expression when they write that the pages are engulfed in raw emotions. Anyone who reads their words from any of their poetic books can always relate to the emotions that they too have felt.

www.ingramcontent.com/pod-product-compliance
Lightning Source LLC
Chambersburg PA
CBHW060923140726
47996CB00001B/360

* 9 7 9 8 2 2 4 1 4 6 8 2 6 *